What Shall We Read Now? : A List Of Books For Children ...

Pratt Institute. Free Library, East Orange Public Library

WHAT SHALL WE READ NOW?

Grades 1 and 2

A LIST OF BOOKS FOR CHILDREN
FROM FOUR TO SEVEN YEARS OLD

Third Edition, Revised

COMPILED BY
THE CHILDREN'S ROOM
PRATT INSTITUTE FREE LIBRARY, BROOKLYN, N. Y.
AND THE
FREE PUBLIC LIBRARY OF EAST ORANGE, N. J.

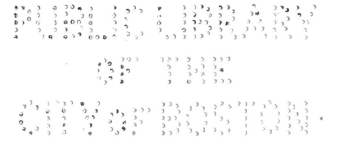
The H. W. Wilson Company
White Plains, N. Y.
1915

GRADES 1 AND 2

PICTURE BOOKS

Adelborg, Ottilia. Clean Peter and the children of Grubbylea Longmans, $1 25

Aldin, Cecil. Happy family. 6v Doran, $ 40 net, each.
Forager.—Humpty and Dumpty —Hungry Peter.—Master Quack—Rags —Rufus
Picture books of pet animals

Brock, H M, illustrator. The old fairy tales. 2v. Warne, $1 00 net each
The first book contains "Puss in boots" and "Jack and the beanstalk," and the second, "Hop o' my thumb" and "Beauty and the beast"

Brooke, L. L. The golden goose book Warne, $2. net.
The stories of The three bears, The three little pigs, The golden goose, and Tom Thumb.

Burgess, Gelett Goops, and how to be them. Stokes, $1.50

Caldecott, Randolph Picture books. 4v Warne, $1 25 each.
Old nursery rhymes and songs.

Cox, Palmer The Brownie books. 9v Century, $1 50 each.

Crane, Walter The baby's bouquet Warne, $1.50 net
——The baby's opera Warne, $1 50 net
Old songs and nursery rhymes set to simple music.
——The baby's own Æsop Warne, $1 50 net
——Picture books 9v Lane, $1 25 each net
Bluebeard's picture book.—Buckle my shoe picture book —Cinderella's picture book —Goody Two Shoes' picture book —Mother Hubbard's picture book —Red Riding Hood's picture book —Song of sixpence picture book.—This little pig's picture book

Deming, E W. Indian child life Stokes, $2 00

Gerson, Virginia. The Happy Heart family. Duffield, $1 25 net

Greenaway, Kate, Marigold garden Warne, $1.50 net.
——The pied piper of Hamelin Warne, $1 50 net.
——Under the window. Warne, $1 50 net.

Lucas, E V Four and twenty toilers, pictures by F. D. Bedford McDevitt-Wilson, $1 75 net

Mother Goose. The big book of nursery rhymes; illustrated by Charles Robinson Dutton, $3.00.
——Jolly Mother Goose annual; illustrated by Blanche Fisher, Wright Rand, $1 25
——Illustrated in color by Kate Greenaway. Warne, $ 60 net.
A quaint little edition which has long been a favorite.
——A nursery rhyme picture book; illustrated by L. Leslie Brooke Warne, $1 00
Paper edition in two books, each $ 50
——The old nursery rhymes; illustrated by Arthur Rackham. Century, $2 50 net.

Our old nursery rhymes; the original tunes harmonized by
Alfred Moffat, illustrated by H. Willebeek Le Mair.
McKay, $1 50 net.
The old nursery songs set to simple melodies for little children to sing.
A second collection is called "Little songs of long ago"

Peary, Mrs J D. Snow baby, a true story with pictures
Stokes, $1 25 net.
About little Marie Ahnighito Peary and the Eskimo children.

Poulsson, Emilie, and **Smith,** Eleanor. Songs of a little
child's day. Bradley, $1 50

STORIES, RHYMES AND "EASY BOOKS"

Baldwin, James. Fairy stories and fables. Am. Bk. Co., $.35
net.

—— Fifty famous stories retold. Am. Bk Co., $.35 net.

Bass, M. F Nature stories for young readers. 2v. Heath,
v. 1, $ 35; v. 2, $ 25 net.
   v 1. Animal life.
   v. 2. Plant life.

Brown, A. F. and **Bell,** J. M. Tales of the red children.
Appleton, $1.00
Indian legends.

Bryant, S. C. The best stories to tell to children. Houghton, $1.50

Burgess, T W. Bedtime story books 8v. Little, $.50 each.
The adventures of Reddy Fox, Johnny Chuck, Peter Rabbit, and the
other little animal folk of the Green Meadows

Chance, L. M. Little folks of many lands. Ginn, $55 net.

Chase, Annie. Buds, stems and roots. Educ. Pub. Co, $ 40
net.

Craik, G. M So-Fat and Mew-Mew. Heath, $.20 net.
Story of a dog and a cat.

Cruikshank, George. The Cruikshank fairy book. Putnam,
$1.25
The stories of Puss in boots, Jack and the bean-stalk, Hop-o-my-thumb
and Cinderella

Dodge, Mrs M. M. Baby days. Century, $1.50

—— New baby world. Century, $1.50
Short stories and rhymes.

—— Rhymes and jingles. Scribner, $1.50

Dopp, K E The tree-dwellers. Rand, $ 45
A simple reader about primitive man.

Dutton, M B World at work. 3v. Am Bk. Co, v. 1, $ 30,
v 2, $.35, v 3, $ 40 net
   v. 1 Fishing and hunting
   v. 2 In field and pasture
   v 3 Trading and exploring.

Grimm Brothers. Fairy tales, edited by Wiltse. 2v Ginn,
$ 35 each net.

Grover, E O Sunbonnet babies in Holland. Rand, $.50

Holbrook, Florence. The Hiawatha primer. Houghton, $.75

Hopkins, W. J The sandman, his farm stories. Page, $1.50

—— The sandman, more farm stories. Page, $1 50
    Stories of a little boy's life on a farm seventy-five years ago.

Lang, Andrew Cinderella Longmans, $.20 net

—— History of Whittington Longmans, $.30 net

—— Jack the Giant-killer. Longmans, $.20 net.

—— Little Red Riding Hood. Longmans, $ 20 net.

—— The nursery rhyme book. Warne, $1 50

—— Prince Darling Longmans, $ 40 net

—— Princess on the glass hill. Longmans, $.30 net.

—— Sleeping Beauty. Longmans, $.20 net.

Lindsay, Maud. Story garden for little children. Lothrop, $1.00

Lucia, Rose. Peter and Polly in summer. Am Bk Co., $.35

Norton, C E. Heart of oak books, v 1-2. Heath, v. 1, $25; v. 2, $35 net
    v. 1. Rhymes, jingles and fables.
    v. 2. Fables and nursery tales.

O'Shea, M V. Six nursery classics Heath, $ 20 net
    CONTENTS —The house that Jack built.—Mother Hubbard —Cock Robin. —Dame Wiggins of Lee —The old woman and her pig —The three bears.

—— Old world wonder stories Heath, $ 20 net
    CONTENTS.—Whittington and his cat.—Jack the Giant-killer.—Tom Thumb —Jack and the bean-stalk.

Perrault, Charles. Tales of Mother Goose. Heath, $ 20 net.
    CONTENTS —Cinderella —The Sleeping Beauty —Little Thumb —Puss in boots —Riquet of the tuft.—Blue Beard —The fairy.—Little Red Riding Hood.

Potter, Beatrix The "Peter Rabbit" books. 14 volumes Warne, $ 50 each.

Poulsson, Emilie. Child stories and rhymes. Lothrop, $1.25

—— Finger plays Lothrop, $1.25

—— Through the farmyard gate Lothrop, $1.25

Pyle, Katharine. Careless Jane. Dutton, $ 75 net.
    Tales in verse.

Richards, Mrs. L. E. Four feet, two feet and no feet. Estes, $2.
    Short stories of "furry and feathery pets"

Scudder, H. E. Fables and folk stories. Houghton, $.75

Shute, K. H, compiler. Land of song. Book I. Silver, $ 36 net
    Poems for the first three grades.

Stevenson, R. L. A child's garden of verses; illustrated by Chas Robinson. Scribner, $1 50

Tileston, Mrs M W. Sugar and spice. Little, $1.25
    Mother Goose rhymes and nursery tales.

Warren, M. L. From September to June with nature. Heath, $ 35 net.

WHAT SHALL WE READ NOW?

Grades 3 and 4

A LIST OF BOOKS FOR CHILDREN
FROM SEVEN TO TEN YEARS OLD

Third Edition, Revised

COMPILED BY
THE CHILDREN'S ROOM
PRATT INSTITUTE FREE LIBRARY, BROOKLYN, N. Y.
AND THE
FREE PUBLIC LIBRARY OF EAST ORANGE, N. J.

The H. W. Wilson Company
White Plains, N. Y.
1915

GRADES 3 AND 4

FAMOUS OLD STORIES AND FAIRY TALES

Æsop. Fables; illustrated by Arthur Rackham Doubleday,
$1 50 net

Andersen, H. C. Fairy tales, translated by Mrs. Lucas
Dutton, $2 50

Babbitt, E C. Jataka tales, retold Century, $1 00 net.

Baldwin, James Old Greek stories Am Bk Co , $ 45 net

—— Thirty more famous stories retold. Am Bk Co , $.50
net

Bible. An old, old story book, by E. M Tappan. Houghton,
$1.50

Bible. Old Testament stories, by Edwin Chisholm. Dutton,
$ 50 net

—— Stories from the life of Christ, by J. H. Kelman. Dutton, $ 50 net.

Brown, A F. The book of saints and friendly beasts.
Houghton, $1 25
About St. Bridget and the king's wolf, St. Keneth of the Gulls, St
Francis, and other saints of long ago

—— In the days of giants, a book of Norse tales. Houghton, $1 10 net

Browne, Frances Granny's wonderful chair and its tales of
fairy times. Heath, $.20 net.

Eastman, C A. Wigwam evenings Little, $1.25
The stories that are told to Indian children

France, Anatole. Honey-Bee; translated by Mrs. John Lane.
Lane, $1 50 net.

Fuller, Eunice The book of friendly giants; illustrated by
Pamela Colman Smith. Century, $2.00 net

Gask, Lilian. Legends of our little brothers Crowell, $1 50

Gibbon, J. M Old King Cole (True annals of fairyland)
Dutton, $1 50
The other volumes are "The reign of King Herla" and "The reign of
King Oberon."

Grimm Brothers Fairy tales; illustrated by Arthur Rackham. Doubleday, $1.50

Harris, J. C. Uncle Remus, his songs and his sayings. Appleton, $2
Stories about "Brer Fox, Brer Rabbit and Mis' Meadows and de gals "

Holbrook, Florence. Book of nature myths. Houghton, $ 65
net.
Tells why the bear has a short tail, and many other wonders.

Jacobs, Joseph. English fairy tales   Putnam, $1.25

Kingsley, Charles.   Water babies, a fairy tale for a land baby   Macmillan, $1. net.

Lagerlöf, Selma.   The wonderful adventures of Nils   Doubleday, $1 35 net.

—— The further adventures of Nils. Doubleday, $1 20 net.

Lang, Andrew. The blue fairy book   Longmans, $1 00 net

—— The green fairy book   Longmans, $1 00 net.

Lummis, C F. Pueblo Indian folk-lore stories. Century, $1 50

MacDonald, George   The light princess, and other fairy tales. Putnam, $1.25 net.

—— The princess and the goblin. Caldwell, $1.50

MacLeod, Mary. Book of King Arthur and his noble knights. Stokes, $1 50

Musset, Paul de   Mr Wind and Madam Rain   Putnam, $2.
A fairy tale of Brittany

Norton, C. E   Heart of oak books. v. 3. Heath, $.40 net.
Fairy tales, narratives and poems.

Pyle, Howard. The wonder clock; four-and-twenty marvellous tales being one for each hour of the day. Harper, $2 00

—— The garden behind the moon   Scribner, $2 00

Roulet, M. F. N. Indian folk tales. Am. Bk. Co., $ 40 net

Ruskin, John. The King of the Golden River. Heath, $.20 net.
The legend of the "Black Brothers"

Scudder, H E. The book of legends. Houghton, $ 50

—— The children's book   Houghton, $2 50
The best old stories, fables and poems

Thackeray, W. M   The rose and the ring, illustrated by Gordon Browne. Stokes, $1.25
A nonsense fairy story.

Thorne-Thomsen, Mrs. Gudrun. East o' the sun and west o' the moon, with other Norwegian folk tales   Row, $.60 net.

Wiggin, K D. and Smith, N. A   The talking beasts. Doubleday, $1.25 net
Fables from many lands

POETRY

Brooke, Leslie. The tailor and the crow. Warne, $1.00 net.
An old nonsense rhyme with pictures.

Edgar, M. G., compiler   A treasury of verse for little children. Crowell, $2 50

Field, Eugene   Lullaby land; illustrated by Chas. Robinson. Scribner, $1.50

Hazard, Bertha, compiler. Three years with the poets; poetry to be memorized during the first years in school. Houghton, $50 net.

Lear, Edward Nonsense books Little, '$2 00

Longfellow, H W. The song of Hiawatha. Houghton, $1.

Lovejoy, M. I., compiler. Nature in verse. Silver, $.60 net.
Poems for spring, summer, autumn and winter

Lucas, E V., compiler. A book of verses for children Holt, $2.00

Riley, J. W. The book of joyous children. Scribner, $1 20 net.

Thaxter, Celia. Stories and poems for children. Houghton, $1 50

Wiggin, Mrs. K D. and **Smith,** N A., compilers The posy ring, a book of verse for children. Doubleday, $1.25 net

STORIES

Alcott, L. M Lulu's library. 3v Little, $1.00 each
Three books of short stories.

Aspinwall, Mrs Alicia Short stories for short people Dutton, $1.50

Barrie, J. M. Peter and Wendy. Scribner, $1 50 net.
The whole story of Peter Pan.

Brown, A. F. The lonesomest doll Houghton, $85 net.

Brown, Alice The one-footed fairy and other stories. Houghton, $1 25 net.

Burgess, Gelett Lively city o' Ligg Stokes, $1 00
A funny book about "the terrible train" and other strange things.

Burnett, Mrs F. H. Racketty-packetty house. Century, $60

Carroll, Lewis. Alice's adventures in wonderland. Macmillan, $1 00 net.

—— Through the looking glass Macmillan, $1 00 net.

Collodi, C. Adventures of Pinocchio Ginn, $.40 net.
How a naughty wooden marionette at last became a real little boy.

Coolidge, Susan. The New-year's bargain. Little, $1 25
Twelve stories, one for each month of the year.

Hale, L. P. The Peterkin papers. Houghton, $1 50
A "funny book."

Harris, J. C Little Mr Thimblefinger and his queer country; what the children saw and heard there Houghton, $2 00

Hopkins, W. J The sandman; his ship stories Page, $1 50
Stories of the brig "Industry"

Howells, W. D Christmas every day, and other stories Harper, $1 25

Jackson, Mrs H. H. Cat stories. Little, $2 00

Jewett, S O Play days. Houghton, $1.50
　Stories for little girls
Lucas, E V., compiler Old fashioned tales Stokes, $1.50
　The stories our great-great-grandfathers read when they were little.
Mulock, D M. The adventures of a brownie Harper, $ 60
—— The little lame prince. Rand, $1 25
Page, T. N Two little Confederates. Scribner, $1.50
　A story of the Civil War.
Paine, A. B. Hollow tree and deep woods book. Harper,
　$1 50
　A "funny book."
Pyle, Katharine. The Christmas angel. Little, $1.25
Richards, Mrs. L E. Five minute stories Estes, $1.25
　Short stories and merry jingles
—— The joyous story of Toto. Little, $1.00
Smith, Mrs M. P. W Jolly good times, or, Child-life on a
　farm. Little, $1.25
Tappan, E. M The house with the silver door. Houghton,
　$1.00 net.
Vimar, Auguste. The curly-haired hen. Fitzgerald, $1.00 net.
　A French nonsense story.
White, E. O When Molly was six. Houghton, $1.

STORIES OF OTHER LANDS AND OLDEN DAYS

Aanrud, Hans. Lisbeth Longfrock Ginn, $ 40 net.
　The story of a little Norwegian girl
Andrews, Jane. Each and all. Ginn, $ 60 net.
—— Seven little sisters. Ginn, $ 60 net.
　Stories of the children in different parts of the world.
—— Ten boys who live on the road from long ago to now
　Ginn, $.60 net
Ayrton, Mrs M. C. Child-life in Japan and Japanese child-
　stories Heath, $.40 net.
Baldwin, James. Fifty famous people. Am. Bk., Co., $ 35 net.
Blaisdell, A. F., and **Ball,** F K. Hero stories from American
　history Ginn, $ 60 net.
Boutet de Monvel, L M. Joan of Arc. Century, $3.00 net
　Beautiful pictures telling the story of the peasant girl who saved
France.
Eggleston, Edward. Stories of American life and adventure
　Am. Bk. Co., $ 50 net.
Holbrook, Florence. Cave, mound and lake dwellers and
　other primitive people. Heath, $ 40 net.
Husted, M. H. Stories of Indian children. Public School
　Pub. Co , $.40 net.

Little cousin series. Page, $ 60 each.

Child-life in many countries, treated in story form. Among the best of the series are Our little Chinese cousin, Our little Swedish cousin, Our little German cousin, Our little Philippine cousin.

O'Neill, Elizabeth. A nursery history of England. Stokes, $2.00 net.

Peary, Mrs J D. Children of the Arctic. Stokes, $1 25 net.

More about the "Snow Baby" and her Eskimo playmates.

Perkins, L F. The Dutch twins. Houghton, $1 00 net

Children who like this will also enjoy her other "twins," the "Japanese," the "Eskimo," and the "Irish twins"

Perry, F. M., and **Beebe,** Katherine. Four American pioneers, Daniel Boone, George Rogers Clark, David Crockett, Kit Carson. Am Bk Co , $.50 net.

Perry, W S. With Azir Girges in Egypt. Atkinson, $.40

Schwatka, Frederick. Children of the cold. Educ. Pub Co , $1 25 net

How the Eskimo children live

Shaw, E R. Big people and little people of other lands. Am. Bk Co , $ 30 net

Spyri, Johanna. Heidi. Ginn, $.40 net.

The story of a little Swiss girl and her mountain home

White, E O. A little girl of long ago. Houghton, $1 00

The life of a little New England girl a hundred years ago.

Zwilgmeyer, Dikken. Johnny Blossom, translated from the Norwegian by Emilie Poulsson. Pilgrim Press, $1 00

OUT-OF-DOOR BOOKS AND ANIMAL STORIES

Andrews, Jane. Stories Mother Nature told her children. Ginn, $ 60 net.

About coal, amber, the frost, seeds and other things.

Bertelli, Luigi. The prince and his ants. Holt, $1 35 net

Ciondolino is the little Italian boy who became an ant and had many adventures with other ants and wasps and bees.

Brown, K. L. The plant baby and its friends; a nature reader for primary grades. Silver, $ 48 net

Burgess, T. W. Mother West Wind's animal stories. Little, $1 00

Claudy, C H. "Tell me why" stories. McBride, $1.25 net

Hardy, M E. Sea stories for wonder eyes. Ginn, $.65 net.

Howes, Edith. The sun's babies. Cassell, $1.25 net

Kelly, M. A. B. Short stories of our shy neighbors. Am Bk. Co , $ 50 net.

Kipling, Rudyard. Just so stories. Doubleday, $1 20 net.

Morley, M W. Little wanderers. Ginn, $ 30 net.

About seeds and plants.

Ségur, comtesse de. Story of a donkey. Heath, $ 20 net.

Strong, F. L. All the year round. 4v. Ginn, $40 each net.
A nature reader for spring, summer, autumn and winter.
Trimmer, Mrs Sarah. History of the robins   Heath, $20 net.

AMUSEMENTS

Beard, Lina, and **Beard,** A. B.   Little folk's handy book.
Scribner, $75 net.
Perry, S. G. S   When mother lets us act.   Moffat, $75 net
Rich, G. E   When mother lets us make paper box furniture.
Moffat, $75 net.
Walker, M. C.   Lady Hollyhock and her friends.   Baker,
$1.25 net
How to make the radish baby, the gingerbread maid, and many other
dolls and toys.

WHAT SHALL WE READ NOW?

Grades 5 and 6

A LIST OF BOOKS FOR CHILDREN FROM TEN TO TWELVE YEARS OLD

Third Edition, Revised

COMPILED BY
THE CHILDREN'S ROOM
PRATT INSTITUTE FREE LIBRARY, BROOKLYN, N. Y.
AND THE
FREE PUBLIC LIBRARY OF EAST ORANGE, N. J.

The H. W. Wilson Company
White Plains, N. Y.
1915

GRADES 5 AND 6

FAMOUS OLD STORIES AND FOLK TALES

Arabian nights entertainments; edited by Andrew Lang
  Longmans, $1.00 net.

Asbjörnsen, P. C. Fairy tales from the far north. Burt, $1 00
  Folk-tales from Norway.

Baldwin, James. The wonder book of horses Century, $.75
  Eighteen stories of winged steeds, of war-horses and heroes

Bunyan, John Pilgrim's progress; illustrated by the brothers Rhead Century, $1.50

Chaucer, Geoffrey Tales of the Canterbury pilgrims; retold by Darton. Stokes, $1 50

Dole, N H., translator. The white duckling and other stories Crowell, $1 00 net

Froissart, Jean. Stories from Froissart; edited by Henry
  Newbolt Macmillan, $1 50 net.
  Stories of chivalry and brave deeds in the days of Edward III and the
Black Prince.

Harris, J. C. Nights with Uncle Remus. Houghton, $1.50
  Myths and legends of the old plantation.

Hawthorne, Nathaniel. A wonder book, illustrated by Walter Crane. Houghton, $3 00

—— Tanglewood tales Houghton, $2.50

Hodges, George. The Garden of Eden; stories from the first
  nine books of the Old Testament. Houghton, $1.50
  There is a second book with more stories called "The Castle of Zion."

Irving, Washington. Rip Van Winkle. Macmillan, $1.50 net.

Jacobs, Joseph. Celtic fairy tales Putnam, $1.25

Laboulaye, Edouard. Fairy tales Dutton, $2 50

Lamb, Charles & Lamb, Mary. Tales from Shakespeare
  Dutton, $2 50

Lang, Andrew. The book of romance. Longmans, $1.00 net.
  About King Arthur and Sir Lancelot, Roland, Robin Hood, and Grettir
the Strong.

MacDonnell, Anne The Italian fairy book. Stokes, $1.35 net.

MacLeod, Mary Stories from the Faerie queene. Stokes,
  $1 50

MacManus, Seumas. Donegal fairy stories. Doubleday, $1.25

Marvin, F. S., and others. Adventures of Odysseus retold in
  English; illustrated by Charles Robinson. Dutton, $1.50
  net.

Nyblom, Helena. Jolly Calle and other Swedish fairy tales;
  illustrated by Charles Folkard. Dutton, $2.50

Pogany, Nander   The Hungarian fairy book. Stokes, $1.35 net

Pyle, Howard. Merry adventures of Robin Hood. Scribner, $3.00.

Steel, Mrs. F. A. Tales of the Punjab. Macmillan, $1 50
How the wily Jackal met his match and other stories told in the villages of India.

Sterling, M. B   The story of Sir Galahad   Dutton, $1 50

Swift, Jonathan   Gulliver's travels, edited by Joseph Jacobs, illustrated by C E Brock (Cranford ed) Macmillan, $1 50 net.

POETRY

Chisholm, Louey, compiler. The golden staircase. Putnam, $1.50

Longfellow, H. W. The children's own Longfellow   Houghton, $1 25

Lovejoy, M I., compiler. Poetry of the seasons   Silver, $.60 net
Nature poems.

Patmore, C K D, compiler   The children's garland   Macmillan, $1.00 net.

Shute, K H., compiler. The land of song. v. 3. Silver, $ 54 net

Thacher, Mrs. L. W., compiler. The listening child   Macmillan, $.50 net.

Tileston, Mrs M W. F, compiler. The children's book of ballads. Little, $1 50
Poems of heroism and adventure.

Whittier, J G., compiler. Child life. Houghton, $1.50

Wiggin, Mrs K D. & Smith, N. A, compilers   Golden numbers   Doubleday, $2 00 net.

LIVES OF FAMOUS MEN AND WOMEN

Baldwin, James. American book of golden deeds. Am. Bk Co , $ 50 net

Brooks, E. S. True story of Christopher Columbus Lothrop, $1.50

—— True story of George Washington   Lothrop, $1 50

Golding, Vautier. The story of David Livingstone. Children's heroes) Dutton, $ 50 net.

Gordy, W. F. American leaders and heroes   Scribner, $ 60

Hodges, George. When the King came. Houghton, $1 20
The story of Christ.

Holland, R. S. Historic inventions. Jacobs, $1.50 net.

Kelly, M. D. The story of Sir Walter Raleigh. (Children's heroes) Dutton, $.50 net

Lang, Andrew. Red book of heroes. Longmans, $1 00, net.
—— The story of Joan of Arc. (Children's heroes.) Dutton, $ 50 net
Lang, Mrs. Andrew The book of saints and heroes. Longmans, $1 00 net
Nicolay, Helen. Boys' life of Abraham Lincoln. Century, $1.50
—— Boys' life of Ulysses S. Grant Century, $1.50
Seawell, M. E. Paul Jones. Appleton, $1.00
Steedman, Amy Knights of art; stories of the early life of great Italian masters. Jacobs $2 00 net

HISTORICAL STORIES AND TALES OF ADVENTURE

Barnes, James. Yankee ships and Yankee sailors; tales of 1812. Macmillan, $1.50 net.
Bourne, H. E. and Benton, E. J. Introductory American history. Heath, $.60 net
Brooks, E. S Master of the Strong Hearts. Dutton, $1 50
   A story of Custer's last rally.
Brooks, Noah. Boy emigrants Scribner, $1 25
   How some boys crossed the Western plains in the days of '49.
—— Boy settlers, early times in Kansas. Scribner, $1.25
Coffin, C. C. Boys of '76. Harper, $2.00
Colonial stories; retold from St. Nicholas. Century, $.65 net.
Defoe, Daniel. Robinson Crusoe, illustrated by the brothers Rhead. Harper, $1 50
Dix, B M. A little captive lad. Macmillan, $1.50 net.
   A story of England in the time of Cromwell.
—— Merrylips Macmillan, $1.50 net.
   England in the days of the cavaliers
Dodge, Mrs M M. The land of pluck Century, $1 50
   About Holland and its people.
Du Chaillu, P. B. Stories of the gorilla country. Harper, $1 25
   Exciting adventures in Africa
Duncan, R B Brave deeds of Revolutionary soldiers Jacobs, $1.50 net
French, H W. Sir Marrok; a tale of the days of King Arthur. Century, $1.00
Hill, C. T Fighting a fire Century, $1 50
   All about the New York Fire Department
Indian stories; retold from St Nicholas. Century, $ 65 net.
Lang, Mrs L. B. The book of princes and princesses. Longmans, $1 00 net
Little people everywhere series. Little, $.60 each.
   Child life and customs of many lands.

Marshall, H E An island story; a child's history of England. Stokes, $2 50 net
"The story tells how the people of Britain grew to be a great people, till the little green island was no longer large enough to contain them all."
—— Scotland's story. Stokes, $2 50 net.
Legendary and true history; Macbeth, Robert the Bruce and many other heroes
Mitton, G. E. Children's book of London. Macmillan, $2.00 net.
Moffett, Cleveland. Careers of danger and daring. Century, $1.80
Peeps at many lands series. Macmillan, $.55 each net.
Readable accounts of many countries, with colored pictures. Among the most interesting are England, Scotland, Germany, Russia, Japan, Burma
Pumphrey, M. B. Stories of the Pilgrims. Rand, $1.00 net.
Pyle, Howard. Otto of the silver hand. Scribner, $2.00
A tale of kidnapping in the old days of robber barons.
Schultz, J. W The quest of the fish-dog skin. Houghton, $1.25 net
An Indian story
Seawell, M. E Little Jarvis. Appleton, $1.00
The story of a boy midshipman and a sea-fight
Steel, Mrs F. A. W. The adventures of Akbar. Stokes, $1 35 net.
A true story of a little prince of India.
Taylor, Bayard Boys of other countries Putnam, $1.25
The "other countries," are Sweden, Egypt, Iceland, Germany and Russia.
True, J. P The iron star and what it saw on its journey through the ages Little, $1.50
Twain, Mark. The prince and the pauper. Harper, $1 75
A story of Edward VI of England.
Wyss, J. D. Swiss family Robinson; illustrated by the brothers Rhead. Harper, $1 50
The story of a family shipwrecked on a desert island.
Yonge, C M. The little duke. Macmillan, $1.25 net.
Richard the Fearless, who became duke of Normandy when he was eight years old

STORIES

Alcott, L M. Eight cousins. Little, $1 50
The story of one girl and her seven boy cousins.
—— Little women; illustrated by A. B. Stephens. Little, $2 00
—— Under the lilacs Little, $1.50
About Ben and Sancho and how they ran away from the circus and found a home in the old house under the lilacs.
Alden, W. L The moral pirates. Harper, $60
The story of four New York boys, and their summer trip up the Hudson.
Aldrich, T. B. The story of a bad boy. Houghton, $1.25

Amicis, Edmondo de Cuore; an Italian schoolboy's journal. Crowell, $.75

Brown, Alice. The secret of the clan. Macmillan, $1.25 net.

Burnett, Mrs F. H The secret garden. Stokes, $1 35 net.

Burton, C P Boy scouts of Bob's Hill. Holt, $1.25 net

Camp, Walter. Danny Fists. Appleton, $1.35 net.

Collidge, Susan. Eyebright Little, $1 25
   The story of a little girl who goes to live on an island off the coast of Maine

—— What Katy did Little, $1.25

Crothers, S. M. Miss Muffet's Christmas party. Houghton, $1 00 net.
   Miss Muffet invited all the story-book people

Diaz, Mrs. A. M. The William Henry letters. Lothrop, $1.00
   Written by a boy at boarding-school.

Dodge, Mrs M. M. Hans Brinker. Scribner, $1.50
   A story of life in Holland.

Dragoumis, J. D. Under Greek skies. Dutton, $1.00 net.
   (Little schoolmates series)
   There are several other volumes in this series about the children of Spain, France, Germany, Scotland and Ireland

Duncan, S. J. Story of Sonny Sahib. Appleton, $1 00
   A story of India.

Ewing, Mrs J H Six to sixteen. (Queens treasures series.) Macmillan, $1.00 net.

Garland, Hamlin. Boy life on the prairie. Macmillan, $1.50

Hall, Mrs F. H. Flossie's play days. Estes, $1 25
   An old-fashioned story.

Jackson, Mrs H. H. Nelly's silver mine Little, $1 50

Jewett, S O Betty Leicester. Houghton, $1 25

Lucas, E. V. Anne's terrible good nature Macmillan, $1 75 net.

MacDonald, George At the back of the North Wind. Caldwell, $1.50
   Almost a fairy tale.

Mason, G S Licky and his gang. Houghton, $1 00 net.

Maynard, Colton. Elliott Gray, jr Grosset, $ 50 net.

Otis, James. Toby Tyler; or, Ten weeks with a circus. Harper, $ 60

Perry, S G S. The kind adventure Stokes, $1 25 net.

Rankin, Mrs. C. W. Dandelion cottage. Holt, $1 50
   A housekeeping story for girls.

Shaw, F. L. Castle Blair. Heath, $ 50 net

Stoddard, W O. Two arrows. Harper, $ 60
   An Indian story.

Wiggin, Mrs. K. D. The Birds' Christmas carol. Houghton, $ 50
   About Carol Bird's Christmas party for the little Ruggleses.

—— Rebecca of Sunnybrook farm. Houghton, $1.25

Wilson, J. F. Tad Sheldon, boy scout. Sturgis, $1.00 net.
Zollinger, Gulielma. Widow O'Callaghan's boys. McClurg, $1 50

OUT-OF-DOOR BOOKS AND ANIMAL STORIES

Bostock, F. C. Training of wild animals Century, $1.00 net
Cat stories; retold from St Nicholas. Century, $ 65 net.
Drummond, Henry. The monkey that would not kill. Dodd, $1.00
Du Chaillu, P. B. The world of the great forest. Scribner, $2 00
Animal life in Africa.
Duncan, Frances When mother lets us garden. Moffat, $.75 net.
Hawkes, Clarence. Piebald, king of bronchos. Jacobs, $1.50
—— Tenants of the trees; illustrated by Louis Rhead. Page, $1.50
Ingersoll, Ernest. Book of the ocean. Century, $1.50
Kipling, Rudyard. The jungle book. Century, $1.50
—— The second jungle book Century, $1.50
Lang, Andrew The book of animal stories. Longmans, $1 00 net
Mitton, G. E. The children's book of stars. Macmillan, $2.00 net.
Morley, M W. The bee people. McClurg, $1.25
Patterson, A. J. The spinner family. McClurg, $1.25
About spiders
Roberts, C. G D Hoof and claw Macmillan, $1 35 net.
Saunders, Marshall. Beautiful Joe Amer. Baptist Pub. Soc , $.50 net.
The autobiography of a dog.
Seton, E. T. Biography of a grizzly. Century, $1 50
—— Wild animals I have known. Scribner, $2 00
Sewell, Anna. Black Beauty; the autobiography of a horse; illustrated by Scrivener Jacobs, $1 00 net.
Stories of brave dogs; retold from St. Nicholas. Century, $ 65 net.
Torelle, Ellen. Plant and animal children. Heath, $ 50 net.

AMUSEMENTS AND OCCUPATIONS

Bailey, C. S. Children's book of games and parties. Donohue, $1.00
Beard, D C. Jack of all trades. Scribner, $2.00
—— The outdoor handy book. Scribner, $2.00

Beard, Lina, and **Beard**, A. B. What **a** girl can make and do. Scribner, $1.60 net.

Beard, Patten, Jolly book of boxcraft. Stokes, $1.35 net.

Burrell, C B. Saturday mornings; or, How Margaret learned to keep house. Estes, $.75

Burroughs, W D. The wonderland of stamps Stokes, $1 50

The games book for boys and **girls.** Dutton, $2 50

Good, Arthur. Magical experiments; or, Science at play McKay, $1.25

Hall, A. N. The boy craftsman. Lothrop, $1 60 net.

Johnson, Constance. When mother lets us cook. Moffat, $.75 net

Levi, Hedwig. Work and play for little girls Duffield, $.75 net.

Lucas, E. V. 300 games and pastimes; or, What shall we do now. Macmillan, $2.00 net.

Mathewson, Christy. Pitching in a pinch. Grosset, $.50 net.

Ralston, Mrs. Virginia. When mother lets us sew. Moffat, $.75 net.

Shafer, D. C. Harper's beginning electricity. Harper, $1.00 net.

Sidgwick, Ethel Four plays for children. Small, $.75 net

Wells, Carolyn. Pleasant day diversions. Moffat, $1.00 net.

WHAT SHALL WE READ NOW?

Grades 7 and 8

A LIST OF BOOKS FOR CHILDREN FROM TWELVE TO FOURTEEN YEARS OLD

Third Edition, Revised

COMPILED BY
THE CHILDREN'S ROOM
PRATT INSTITUTE FREE LIBRARY, BROOKLYN, N. Y.
AND THE
FREE PUBLIC LIBRARY OF EAST ORANGE, N. J.

The H. W. Wilson Company
White Plains, N. Y.
1915

GRADES 7 AND 8

FAMOUS OLD STORIES, LEGENDS AND FOLKLORE

Baldwin, James   Story of Roland   Scribner, $1.50
  Daring feats of the great baron of France and his companions in arms.
—— Story of Siegfried   Scribner, $1 50
  How the Nibelungen hero forged his wondrous sword, rode through flaming fire to awaken Brunhild, and did many daring deeds
—— The story of the Golden Age.   Scribner, $1 50
  Greek legends relating to the causes of that great Trojan War about which Homer wrote in the "Iliad" and Odyssey."
Buckley, E F.   Children of the dawn; old tales of Greece   Stokes, $1 50
Cervantes Saavedra, Miguel de.   Don Quixote; retold by Judge Parry, illustrated by Walter Crane.   Lane, $1 50
  Strange and amusing adventures of the Spanish knight-errant, who fights windmills
Chapin, A A.   Konigskinder   Harper, $1 25
  A fairy tale founded on Humperdinck's fairy opera.
Cuchulain.   The boy's Cuchulain; heroic legends of Ireland, by Eleanor Hull.   Crowell, $1.50 net
Grinnell, G. B   Blackfoot Lodge tales.   Scribner, $1.75 net.
  Indian stories told by Indians
Guerber, H. M. A.   Stories of the Wagner opera.   Dodd, $1 50
  Legends of the Flying Dutchman, the Ring of the Nibelungen, and others, as Wagner used them in his operas.
Homer.   Stories from Homer, by A J Church.   Dodd, $1.25 net.
Irving, Washington.   The sketch book   Putnam, $1 50
  Contains Rip Van Winkle, The legend of Sleepy Hollow, Christmas, etc
Kingsley, Charles.   The heroes   Dutton, $2 50
  Stories of Perseus and the Gorgon, Theseus and the Minotaur, Jason and the golden fleece.
La Motte-Fouqué, baron de   Undine, illustrated by Arthur Rackham   Doubleday, $2 50 net
  Romantic tale of a water nymph who married a knight.
Mabie, H W   Norse stories retold from the Eddas   Dodd, $1 80 net.
  The old stories of Loki and his misdoings, of Tyr and the Fenris-wolf, of Odin and Thor and Baldur the Beautiful
Plummer, M. W   Stories from the chronicle of the Cid.   Holt, $.90 net.
  Adventures of the great Cid Campeador of Spain, most wonderful of heroes, who was never defeated.
Plutarch.   Plutarch's Lives for boys and girls, retold by W. H. Weston.   Stokes, $1 50 net

Pyle, Howard The story of King Arthur and his knights. Scribner, $2.00 net.

The other three books are The story of Sir Launcelot and his companions, The story of the Champions of the Round Table, and The Story of the Grail and the passing of Arthur.

Quiller-Couch, A. T. Historical tales from Shakespeare. Scribner, $1.50

Raspe, R. E. Tales from the travels of Baron Munchausen, edited by E. E Hale. Heath, $.20 net.

"How the baron drove a wolf in harness; how a lion jumped into a crocodile's mouth, and how the baron's cloak went mad."

Spenser, Edmund. Una and the Red cross knight, and other tales from Spenser's Faery queene; by N. G. Royde-Smith. Dutton, $2.50

POETRY

Gilder, J. L., compiler. The heart of youth. Sturgis, $1.25 net.

Henley, W. E., compiler. Lyra heroica; a book of verse for boys. Scribner, $1 25 net.

Longfellow, H. W. Complete poetical works (Cambridge ed.) Houghton, $2.00

Macaulay, T. B. Lays of ancient Rome. Longmans, $1.25

Maeterlinck, Maurice. The blue bird. Dodd, $1.20 net.

The play which tells the adventures of Tyltyl and Mytyl in their search for the "Blue Bird of Happiness"

Percy, Thomas, compiler. The boys' Percy; from Pency's Reliques of ancient English poetry; edited for boys by Sidney Lanier Scribner, $2 00

Stirring ballads of the old days of English border warfare and chivalry.

Scott, Sir Walter. Poetical works. (Globe ed.) Macmillan, $1.75 net.

Tennyson, Alfred. Poetical works (Globe ed.) Macmillan, $1.75 net.

Wells, Carolyn, compiler. A nonsense anthology. Scribner, $1.25

Wiggin, Mrs K. D., and **Smith**, N. A., compilers. Golden numbers. Doubleday, $2.00 net.

BIOGRAPHY

Bangs, M R. Jeanne d'Arc Houghton, $1 25 net

The true story of the life of Joan the Maid, who led the king's armies to victory

Bruce, H A. Daniel Boone and the wilderness road. Macmillan, $1.50 net.

Eastman, C. A Indian boyhood. Doubleday, $1 60 net.

Dr. Eastman's own boyhood. He is a full-blooded Sioux.

Frothingham, J. P. Sea fighters from Drake to Farragut Scribner, $1.20 net.

Gilbert, Ariadne. More than conquerors Century, $1.25 net.
Biography of noble men, Lincoln, Walter Scott, Phillips Brooks and many others

Hill, F. T. On the trail of Grant and Lee Appleton, $1 50 net
An interesting book about two of our great generals

Johnston, C. H L Famous frontiersmen and heroes of the border Page, $1 50

Keller, Helen. The story of my life. Doubleday, $1 50 net
How Helen Keller, the little blind and deaf girl, learned to read and speak, made many friends, and afterward went through college

Meadowcroft, W. H Boy's life of Edison Harper, $1 25
Every boy who has a liking for electrical matters will enjoy this book about the great wizard of electricity.

Morgan, James Abraham Lincoln, the boy and the man Grosset, $ 75

Moses, Belle Louisa May Alcott Appleton, $1 25 net.

Richards, Mrs. L E. Florence Nightingale. Appleton, $1.25 net.
The story of the famous English nurse who taught the world what nursing the sick and wounded means

Rolfe, W J Shakespeare the boy Harper, $1 25
His native town and neighborhood, his home life, school, games and sports

Scudder, H E George Washington Houghton, $ 75

Seelye, Mrs. E E The story of Columbus Appleton, $1 75

Tappan, E. M. The Christ story Houghton. $1 50

Washington, B. T. Up from slavery Doubleday. $1.50 net.
How Booker Washington, a little slave boy, grew to be the foremost colored citizen of the United States

BOOKS ABOUT THE UNITED STATES

Abbot, W. J The story of our army for young Americans. Dodd, $2 00 net
There is a similar book called "The story of our navy"

Bishop, Farnham. Panama, past and present Century, $ 75 net.

Du Puy, W. A. Uncle Sam, wonder worker Stokes, $1 25 net
Tells of some of the "big things" our government is doing to make living conditions better for its citizens. Continued in "Uncle Sam's modern miracles"

Famous adventures and prison escapes of the civil war Century, $1 50

Fiske, John. The war of independence. Houghton, $.75

Grinnell, G. B. The story of the Indian Appleton, $1.50
—— Trails of the pathfinders Scribner, $1 50 net
About Lewis and Clark, Fremont and the other early explorers of the Great West

Gordy, W. F. American beginnings in Europe. Scribner, $.75 net

Marriott, Crittenden, Uncle Sam's business. Harper, $1.25
How our government is conducted.

Parkman, Francis. The Oregon trail. Little, $2 00
A picture of the true Indian of the plains, as he was when Parkman hunted buffalo in the Black Hills nearly seventy years ago.

Rolt-Wheeler, Francis The boy with the U S explorers. Lothrop, $1.50
Other volumes in the series tell of the work of the U. S foresters, the U S census, the U S. fisheries, the U. S. survey, and the U S. Indians.

Stevens, W. O. The story of our navy. Harper, $1 50 net

Stockton, F. R. Buccaneers and pirates of our coasts. Macmillan, $1 50 net.

HISTORICAL STORIES (UNITED STATES)

Andrews, Mrs M R. S. The perfect tribute Scribner, $.50 net.
Story of Lincoln and a Confederate soldier boy.

Bennett, John. Barnaby Lee Century, $1 50
Barnaby escapes from pirates and reaches New Amsterdam in the days of Peter Stuyvesant

Churchill, Winston Richard Carvel. Macmillan, $1.50 net.
A stirring tale of Revolutionary times

Cooper, J. F. The last of the Mohicans; illustrated by Boyd Smith. Holt, $1.35 net
During the French and Indian wars.

Fox, John, jr. The little shepherd of Kingdom come Scribner, $1 50
The civil war period.

Hale, E. E. The man without a country Little, $.75
"The effect of Burr's treason on a young naval officer."

Jackson, Mrs. H. H Ramona Little, $1 50
A story of the wrongs suffered by the Indians.

Mitchell, S. W Hugh Wynne. Century, $1 50
A story of revolutionary times in Philadelphia.

Sabin, E L. On the plains with Custer. Lippincott, $1.25 net.
A story which ends with the battle of the Little Big Horn

HISTORY OF OTHER COUNTRIES

Coxhead, Margaret Mexico Stokes, $2 00. (Romance of history series.)
There are other volumes about Australia, Canada, The Netherlands, India, Gibraltar and the West Indies, New Zealand, South Africa and West Africa.

Griffis, W E. Young people's history of Holland Houghton, $1 50

Lang, Andrew. The red true story book. Longmans, $2.00

Marshall, H. E India's story. Stokes, $ 75
There are similar volumes about Canada, Australasia and South Africa.

Platt, William, **and Platt**, Mrs. William. Stories of the Scottish border. Crowell, $1.50

Tappan, E. M. In the days of Alfred the Great. Lothrop, $1.00

Van Bergen, Robert. The story of Japan. Am. Bk. Co., $.60 net.

LIFE AND ADVENTURE IN MANY LANDS

Bond, A. R. With the men who do things. Munn, $1.50 net.
How two boys learned about skyscrapers, battleships, sand-hogs, submarines, etc. Their further adventures are told in "Pick, shovel, and pluck."

Bennett, John. Master Skylark. Century, $1.50.
A tale of Shakespeare's times, in the reign of Queen Elizabeth.

Collins, F. A. The wireless man; his work and adventures on land and sea. Century, $1.20 net.

Du Chaillu, P. B Wild life under the equator. Harper, $1.25
Stories of the African forest.

Duncan, Norman. Adventures of Billy Topsail. Revell, $1.50
Exciting stories of Labrador life

Ford, J. L. The third alarm; a story of the New York Fire Department. Brentano, $1.25

French, H. W The lance of Kanana; a story of Arabia. Lothrop, $1.00
Kanana was a brave Bedouin boy.

Greely, A. W. True tales of Arctic heroism in the new world. Scribner, $1 50 net.

Grenfell, W. T. Adrift on an icepan. Houghton, $75
A thrilling escape from the Labrador sea

Kingsley, Charles. Westward ho! Macmillan, $1.00 net
"Voyages and adventures of Sir Amyas Leigh in the reign of her most glorious majesty, Queen Elizabeth."

Kipling, Rudyard. Captains courageous. Century, $1 50
How a rich boy falls overboard from an Atlantic liner, is picked up by fishermen, and has to work out his passage to the fishing banks and home again.

—— Kim Doubleday, $1.35
A story of India.

Landor, A. H. S. An explorer's adventures in Tibet Harper, $1.50

London, Jack. The call of the wild. Macmillan, $1 50
A dog story of the Klondike.

Masefield, John, Jim Davis. Stokes, $1 25
Wild adventures of a small Devonshire boy with smugglers on the English coast a hundred years and more ago.

Porter, Jane. The Scottish chiefs; illustrated by Robinson. Dutton, $2 00
A thrilling romance of the adventurous times of Robert the Bruce.

Pyle, Howard. Men of iron. Harper, $2 00
A tale of the deeds of Myles Falworth, created knight by his majesty Henry IV of England

Scott, Sir Walter. Ivanhoe. Lippincott, $1 75
  In this story of the tournament at Ashby, Robin Hood is one of the characters, under the name of Locksley the Yeoman

—— Quentin Durward. (Dryburgh ed.) Macmillan, $1.25 net.
  Exciting adventures of a young Scot in France in the 15th century.

Stevenson, R. L. The black arrow. Scribner, $1.25
  A tale of the Wars of the Roses; what happened to Richard Shelton and the outlaw band of the "Black arrow."

—— Treasure island. Scribner, $1 25
  An exciting search for hidden treasure.

White, Claude Graham-, and **Harper,** Harry. Heroes of the air. Doran, $1.50 net.

STORIES

Alcott, L M. Jack and Jill. Little, $1.50
  The story of a boy and girl comradeship

Atkinson, E S. Greyfriars Bobby. Harper, $1.20
  A Scotch story of a dog

Barrie, J M The little minister. Crowell, $1.50
  A Scotch story, of which the heroine is Babbie, who pretends to be a gypsy girl

Blackmore, R. D. Lorna Doone. Crowell, $1.50
  A romance of Exmoor, which includes the story of the savage deeds of the outlaw Doones.

Dickens, Charles. A Christmas carol. Dutton, $1 00

—— David Copperfield. 2v. (Centenary ed) Scribner, $2.00 net.

—— A tale of two cities. (Centenary ed.) Scribner, $1.00 net
  The time of the French revolution.

Dodge, Mrs. M. M. Donald and Dorothy. Century, $1 50
  A sixteen-year-old brother and sister.

Hornung, E. W Fathers of men Scribner, $1.30 net.
  An English school story for boys who like "Tom Brown's schooldays "

Hughes, Thomas. Tom Brown's school days. (Cranford ed) Macmillan, $2 00 net.
  A story of English school life at Rugby.

Johnson, Owen. The varmint. Baker, $1.50
  A story of Lawrenceville school.

Pier, A. S Harding of St Timothy's. Houghton, $1.50

Stuart, Mrs R. M. Story of Babette Harper, $1.50
  A little Creole girl who was stolen by a gypsy from her home in New Orleans.

Twain, Mark. The adventures of Tom Sawyer. Harper, $1.75

Vaile, Mrs. C. M. The Orcutt girls. Wilde, $1 50
  School experiences of two girls in a New England academy.

Wiggin, Mrs. K. D. Mother Carey's chickens Houghton, $1.25 net.

OUT-OF-DOOR BOOKS AND OUTDOOR SPORTS

Beard, Lina, and **Beard,** A. B   Girl pioneers of America
  National Americana Society, $.35 net.
Boy Scouts of America. Official handbook for boys   Gros-
  set, $ 50 net
The **Camp Fire Girls.**   The book of the Camp Fire Girls.
  Camp Fire Girls, $.25 net.
Claudy, C H. The battle of baseball   Century, $1.50 net
Dana, Mrs F T   According to season   Scribner, $1 75 net
    About the wild flowers at different times of year
Ingersoll, Ernest   Wild neighbors   Macmillan, $1 50 net.
    The squirrel, panther, coyote, porcupine, skunk, etc
Martin, E C   Our own weather   Harper, $1 25
    Interesting explanation of the air-currents, the winds and clouds;
  storms and how they are foretold.
Martin, M. E   The friendly stars   Harper, $1 25 net
Miller, O T   The first book of birds   Houghton, $ 60 net
Price, O W   The land we live in; the boys' book of con-
  servation   Small, $1 50 net.
Rogers, J. E. Trees that every child should know   Double-
  day, $1 20 net
Seton, E T. The book of woodcraft   Doubleday, $1 75 net
Sharp, D. L   A watcher in the woods   Century, $ 84 net.
Weed, C. M. Nature biographies. Doubleday, $1 35 net
    "Lives of some every day butterflies, moths, grasshoppers and flies."

OCCUPATIONS AND HANDICRAFT

Adams, J. H   Harper's machinery book for boys. Harper,
  $1.50 net.
Armstrong, D. B   The boys' book of stamp collecting
  Stokes, $1 75 net
Beard, D C   Field and forest handy book; new ideas for
  out of doors. Scribners, $2 00
Collins, F. A   The boys' book of model areoplanes   Cen-
  tury, $1 20 net
Davis, C G, editor. Harper's boating book for boys   Har-
  per, $1.75
Hall, A. N. Handicraft for handy boys. Lothrop, $2.00 net.
Kelley, L E   Three hundred things a bright girl can do.
  Estes, $1.75
    Suggestions for entertainments, clubs, and ways of earning money
Lounsberry, Alice   The garden book for young people
  Stokes, $1 50
St. John, T M   How two boys made their own electrical
  apparatus. St. John, $1.00
Verrill, A H   Harper's aircraft book   Harper, $1 00 net.
—— Harper's wireless book   Harper, $1 00 net.

CPSIA information can be obtained
at www.ICGtesting.com
Printed in the USA
LVHW09s2134300718
585448LV00015B/219/P

9 781247 118611